Pet Cat, Big Cat

Written by Alison Hawes

I am a cat. I am a pet.

I can run and jump.

I sit in the sun a lot.

I hiss and spit if I am cross.

I hunt in the grass.

I drink milk. I lap it up.

I am a big cat. I am not a pet.

I can run fast.

I sit in the sun a lot.

I hiss and spit if I am cross.

I hunt in the grass.

I jump in the pond if it is hot.

Pet cats

Big cats

Ideas for reading

Learning objectives: Extend vocabulary, exploring the meanings and sounds of new words; Hear and say sounds in words in the order in which they occur; Understanding how information can be found in non-fiction texts to answer question; Use talk to organise, sequence and clarify thinking, ideas, feelings, events.

Curriculum links: Knowledge and understanding of the world: find out about, and identify some features of living things;

Look closely at similarities and differences, patterns and change.

Focus phonemes: i (sit, in, hiss), c (cat, cross), h (hunt, hiss), l (lot, lap)

Other new phonemes: s, a, t, p, n, k, e, o, r, m, d, g, u, h, f, b

Fast words: I, a, the

Word Count: 83

Getting started

- Do some fast-reading using a small whiteboard. Write the words that feature the focus phonemes *i, c, h* and *l* on the whiteboard and ask the group to read them, blending aloud if they need to.

- Write up the words *hiss* and *spit* on a whiteboard. If necessary, demonstrate blending the words and then ask the children: *Which animals do you know that hiss and spit when they are cross?* Invite children to act out this behaviour and then ask them to show how cats behave when they are happy.

- Read the title of the book together, blending along the words. Looking at the front cover only, ask: *What is the same about these two cats? What could be different?* Ask the group to say what they think this book is going to teach them.

Reading and responding

- Hand out copies of the book for the children to read independently. Listen in as individuals read. Where necessary, discuss the words *hunt, drink, milk* and *lap.*